The Nervous System

By Simon Rose

MEDIA ENHANCED BOOKS
AV2 BY WEIGL™
ADDED VALUE • AUDIO VISUAL

www.av2books.com

AV² provides enriched content that supplements and complements this book. Weigl's AV² books strive to create inspired learning and engage young minds in a total learning experience.

Your AV² Media Enhanced books come alive with...

 Audio
Listen to sections of the book read aloud.

 Key Words
Study vocabulary, and complete a matching word activity.

 Video
Watch informative video clips.

 Quizzes
Test your knowledge.

Go to www.av2books.com, and enter this book's unique code.

BOOK CODE

M 7 1 0 1 8 3

 Embedded Weblinks
Gain additional information for research.

 Slide Show
View images and captions, and prepare a presentation.

AV² by Weigl brings you media enhanced books that support active learning.

 Try This!
Complete activities and hands-on experiments.

... and much, much more!

Published by AV² by Weigl
350 5th Avenue, 59th Floor
New York, NY 10118
Websites: www.av2books.com www.weigl.com

Library of Congress Cataloging in Publication Data Available on Request

ISBN 978-1-4896-1174-1 (hardcover)
ISBN 978-1-4896-1175-8 (softcover)
ISBN 978-1-4896-1176-5 (single-user eBook)
ISBN 978-1-4896-1177-2 (multi-user eBook)

Printed in the United States of America in North Mankato, Minnesota
1 2 3 4 5 6 7 8 9 0 18 17 16 15 14

062014
WEP090514

Project Coordinator Aaron Carr
Art Director Terry Paulhus

Photo Credits
Every reasonable effort has been made to trace ownership and to obtain permission to reprint copyright material. The publishers would be pleased to have any errors or omissions brought to their attention so that they may be corrected in subsequent printings.

Weigl acknowledges Getty Images as its primary image supplier for this title.

Contents

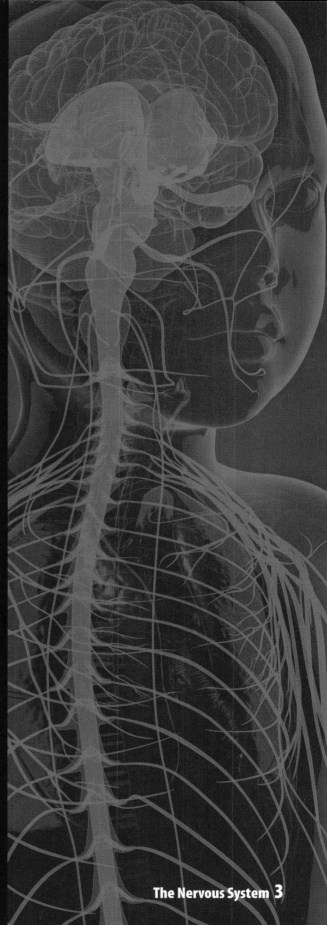

AV² Book Code 2

Human Body Systems 4

What Is the Nervous System? 6

Nervous System Features 8

How Does the Nervous System Work? 10

The Brain 12

The Spinal Cord 14

The Torso and Neck 16

Arms, Hands, Legs, and Feet 18

Keeping Healthy 20

Studying the Nervous System 22

Working Together 24

Careers 26

The Nervous System Quiz 28

Activity 30

Key Words/Index 31

Log on to www.av2books.com 32

Human Body Systems

The human body is made up of many complex systems. Each one plays an important role in how the body works. The systems also work together to help the body function.

For the body to remain healthy, the systems all need to work together properly. Problems or diseases in one body system can have an effect on one or more of the others. More severe problems are likely to affect a larger number of different systems.

6 MAJOR BODY SYSTEMS

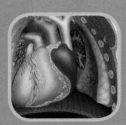

CARDIOVASCULAR SYSTEM

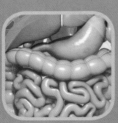

DIGESTIVE SYSTEM

MUSCULAR SYSTEM

NERVOUS SYSTEM

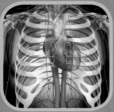

RESPIRATORY SYSTEM

SKELETAL SYSTEM

NERVOUS SYSTEM

Includes the brain, **sensory organs**, spinal cord, and nerves that connect to the rest of the body

Has two main parts, the central nervous system and the peripheral nervous system

Sends messages back and forth between the brain and the body

Contains specialized **cells** called neurons that make up nerves

Regulates internal **organs** and various body processes, such as blood pressure

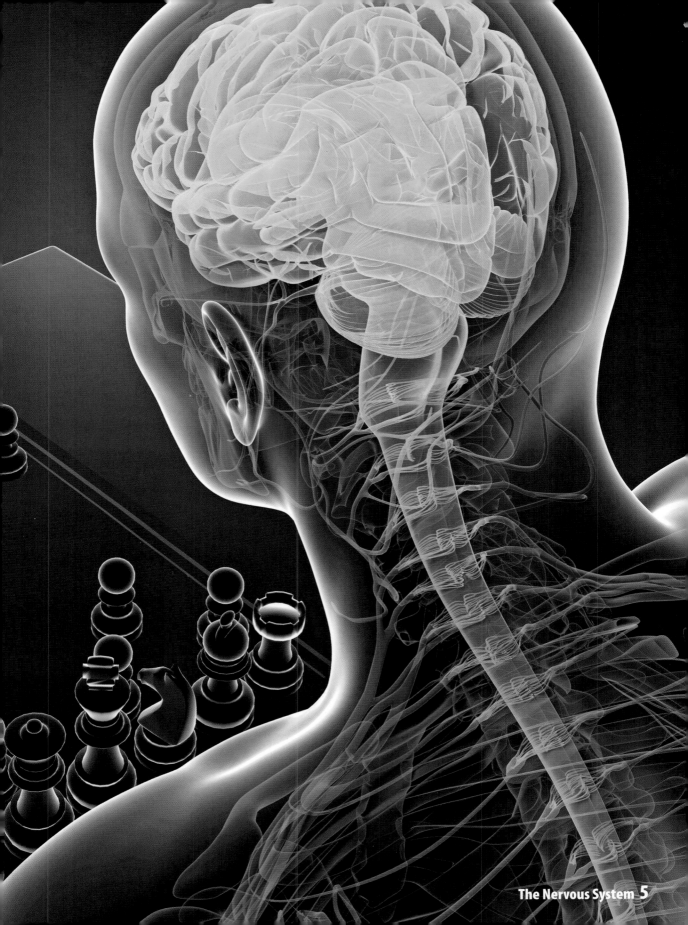

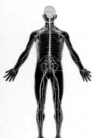

What Is the Nervous System?

The brain and the spinal cord make up the central nervous system. The rest of the nerves and the sensory organs form the body's peripheral nervous system. Working together, the two main areas of the nervous system help the different parts of the body communicate with one another.

The autonomic nervous system is part of the peripheral nervous system. It regulates internal organs such as the heart, intestines, and stomach. The entire nervous system works with the brain to control what is happening throughout the body. The central nervous system gathers information from the senses. The spinal cord takes this information to the brain. Based on the information it receives, the brain gives instructions to parts of the body to perform certain functions. These messages travel through the spinal cord and other nerves to the areas of the body that need to receive them.

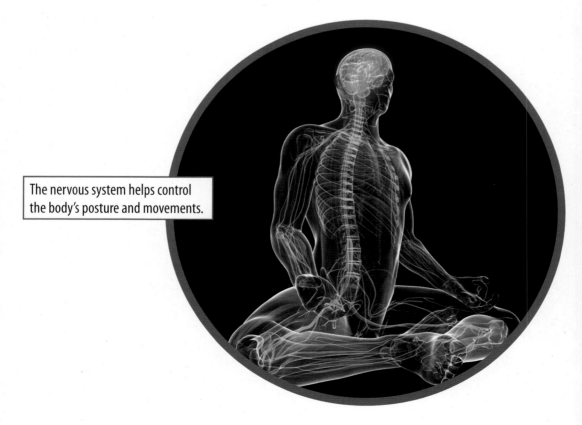

The nervous system helps control the body's posture and movements.

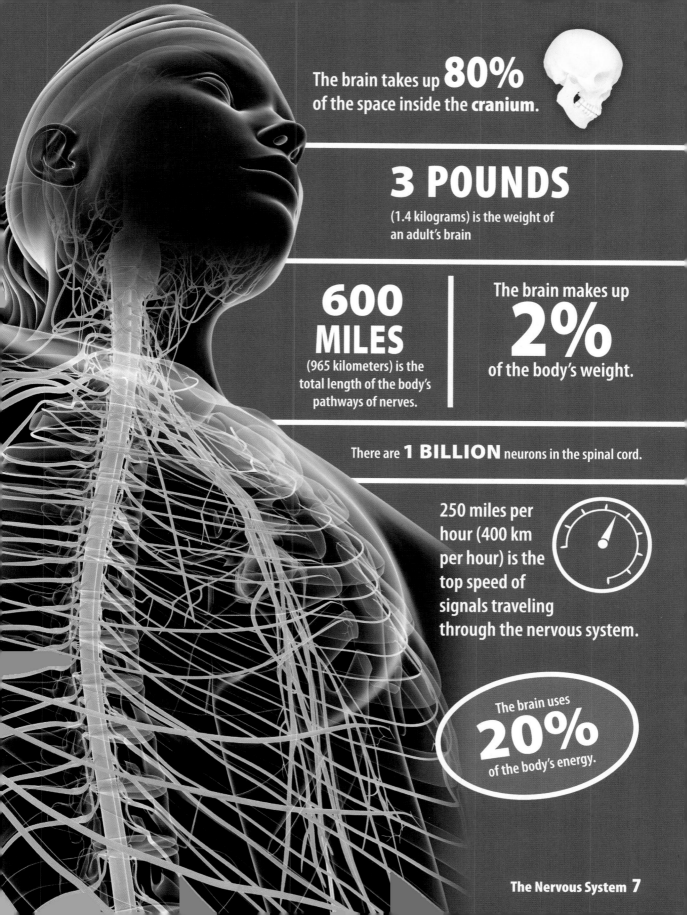

The brain takes up **80%** of the space inside the **cranium**.

3 POUNDS

(1.4 kilograms) is the weight of an adult's brain

600 MILES

(965 kilometers) is the total length of the body's pathways of nerves.

The brain makes up **2%** of the body's weight.

There are **1 BILLION** neurons in the spinal cord.

250 miles per hour (400 km per hour) is the top speed of signals traveling through the nervous system.

The brain uses **20%** of the body's energy.

Nervous System Features

Within the nervous system, nerves use electrical signals to send messages to and from the brain.

CENTRAL NERVOUS SYSTEM The brain contains about 100 billion neurons.

PERIPHERAL NERVOUS SYSTEM Nerves in the peripheral nervous system are made up of bundles of neurons.

CEREBROSPINAL FLUID A clear fluid surrounds the organs of the central nervous system.

MENINGES The meninges form thin protective coverings around the parts of the central nervous system.

NEURONS Nerve cells include a central portion, called the nucleus or cell body, and strands that carry electrical signals.

NEUROGLIA Also called glial cells, the neuroglia protect and feed neurons.

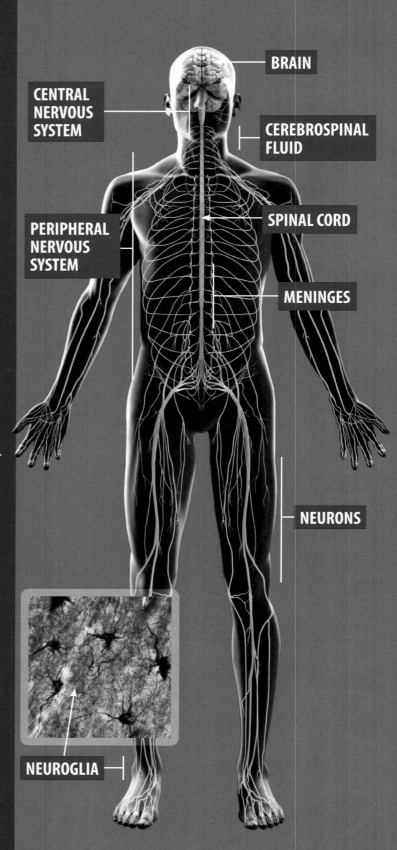

BRAIN

CENTRAL NERVOUS SYSTEM

CEREBROSPINAL FLUID

SPINAL CORD

PERIPHERAL NERVOUS SYSTEM

MENINGES

NEURONS

NEUROGLIA

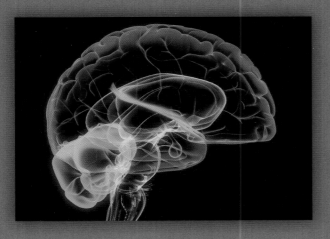

Brain

The brain is the most important part of the nervous system. It is responsible for people's higher mental functions but also helps to control breathing, digestion, and the rate at which the heart beats.

Spinal Cord

The spinal cord runs from the brain down the back of the **torso**. It is inside the spinal column. This series of connected bones, called vertebrae, protects the spinal cord from injury.

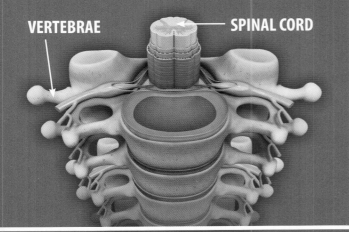

VERTEBRAE SPINAL CORD

Nerves

The **connective tissue** around nerves both protects them and speeds up the rate at which messages can travel.

Sensory Organs

In sensory organs such as the eyes, ears, and nose, nerves gather information to send to the brain. Nerves throughout the body send information to the brain about sensations such as heat, cold, pressure, and pain.

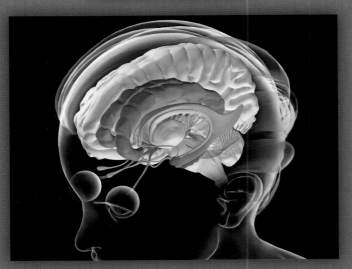

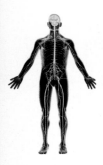

How Does the Nervous System Work?

The brain can be thought of as a central computer that controls the body's functions. Different types of neurons provide information to the brain and transmit messages the brain sends out. Sensory, or afferent, neurons receive information from the eyes, ears, nose, tongue, and skin and send this data to the brain. Motor, or efferent, neurons carry messages away from the brain to the rest of the body. For example, when someone steps on a sharp object, sensory neurons in the foot's skin transmit a pain message to the brain. The brain sends a message back at very high speed, telling the muscles in the foot to pull away from the source of the pain.

The senses are vital to the operation of the nervous system. The brain processes the information that sensory organs receive. For example, when light enters the eye, it reaches a structure at the back of the eye called the retina. The retina changes that light into electrical signals, which are carried to the brain by the optic nerve. The brain then interprets what the eye sees. When sound waves enter the ears, the eardrums vibrate. These vibrations travel through the ear and are converted into electrical signals carried to the brain. The brain then tells the person what he or she is hearing. Taste buds are small sensory organs on the tongue that react to bitter, salty, sour, or sweet sensations. Messages about these tastes travel to the brain, which processes them.

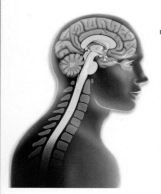

The Role of the Nervous System

SENSE The nervous system collects information about what is happening in and around the body.

PROCESS The brain processes the information sent to it by neurons throughout the body.

ACT Based on the information it receives, the brain sends signals to the body to perform specific functions.

Diagram of a Nervous System Pathway

The spinal cord is the nervous system's main pathway for messages traveling to and from the brain. Nerves that are part of the peripheral nervous system branch out from the spinal cord. They extend to organs and **tissues** in all parts of the body.

A pain message from a sensory neuron travels up neurons in peripheral nerves to the spinal cord. Then, the spinal cord relays the message up to the brain.

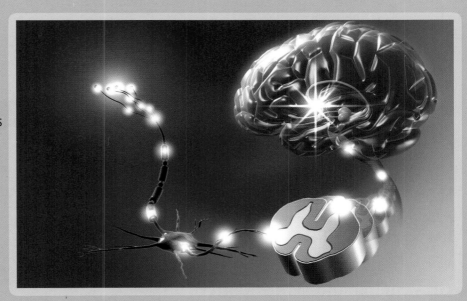

AXON

CELL BODY

DENDRITE

SYNAPSE

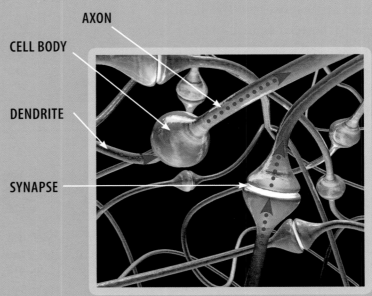

PARTS OF A NEURON

The strands of neurons that carry messages to the cell body are called dendrites. The strands that take signals from the cell body to the next neuron are named axons. Electrical signals cross small spaces between neurons. These spaces are called synapses.

DIRECTION OF MESSAGE • • • • ▶

The Brain

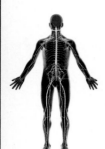

The bones of the skull protect the brain. It is also protected by cerebrospinal fluid. The major brain parts are the cerebrum, cerebellum, and brainstem.

The cerebrum is the largest area of the brain. It controls thinking, understanding, and movement. The cerebellum is located in back of the cerebrum and is much smaller. It controls balance and coordination, or how well muscles work together. The brainstem is the part of the brain that connects to the spinal cord. It sends messages controlling how various organs function. For example, it signals the lungs to breathe.

Above the brainstem is the thalamus. It helps process sensory information. It also controls sleep and alertness. The hypothalamus is at the base of the brain. It produces a number of **hormones** that help the body function properly.

Gray Matter and White Matter

The brain areas closest to the skull are called gray matter because of their color. Gray matter is darkened by neuron cell bodies. Brain parts with more nerve cell strands are lighter in color. These areas are called white matter.

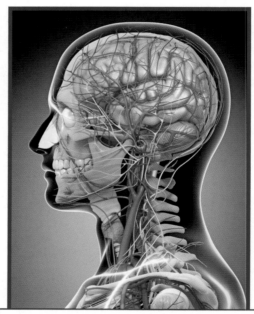

Many blood vessels supply the brain with energy.

The BRAIN by the Numbers	**85**	**5**	**1/10**
	The cerebrum makes up about 85 percent of the brain.	Five areas of the brain control how the body functions.	The cerebellum is one-tenth the size of the cerebrum.

Diagram of the Brain

The left and right halves to the brain have different functions. The left side of the brain controls the right half of the body, and the right side controls the left half. The left side is also concerned with language, including speaking and understanding words that are heard. In addition, the left side controls logic and math calculations. The left side retrieves facts from the memory, as well. The right half of the brain understands pictures, recognizes faces, and processes some types of sounds, including music.

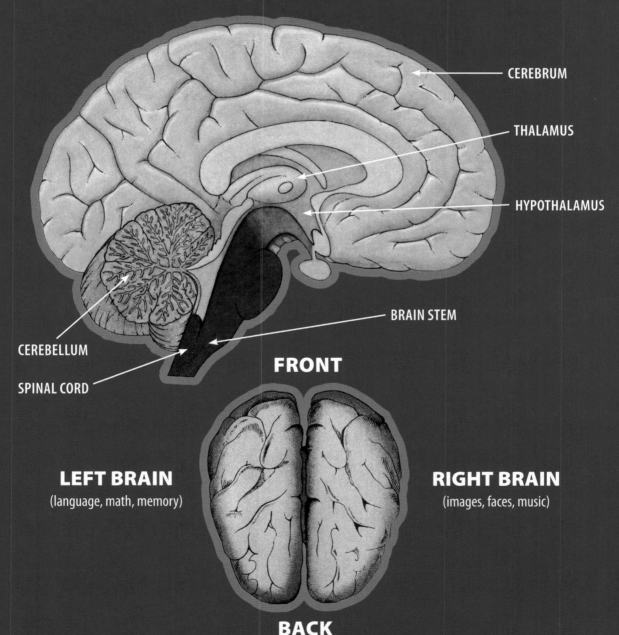

CEREBRUM

THALAMUS

HYPOTHALAMUS

BRAIN STEM

CEREBELLUM

SPINAL CORD

FRONT

LEFT BRAIN
(language, math, memory)

RIGHT BRAIN
(images, faces, music)

BACK

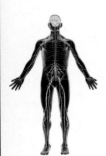

The Spinal Cord

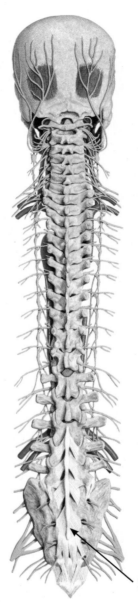

The spinal cord begins at the medulla oblongata, which is the lower part of the brainstem. The cord runs down the center of the back from the neck to the lower back. Like the brain, the spinal cord has gray matter and white matter. In the spinal cord, however, the white matter surrounds the gray matter.

Two Pathways

The spinal cord is a bundle of nerves that is shaped like a cylinder, or tube. The nerves send signals in two pathways, known as tracts. Ascending nerve tracts carry information up from the body to the brain. Descending tracts send information in the opposite direction.

> In the lower part of the spinal column, some of the vertebrae are fused, or joined together. This area is called the sacrum. The fused vertebrae make the spinal column less flexible but help protect the spinal cord.

SACRUM

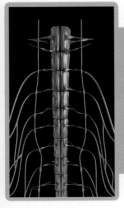

The SPINAL CORD by the Numbers

17–18	31	0.5–0.25
An adult's spinal cord length is 17–18 inches (43–46 centimeters).	There are 31 pairs of nerves extending from the spinal cord.	The width of the spinal cord is 0.5–0.25 inches (1.3–0.6 cm).

Diagram of the Spinal Cord

The 31 pairs of nerves, known as spinal nerves, that extend from the spinal cord are grouped according to the area where they are located. There are eight pairs of cervical nerves in the neck. They are followed by twelve pairs of thoracic nerves, five pairs of lumbar nerves, five pairs of sacral nerves, and one pair of coccygeal nerves.

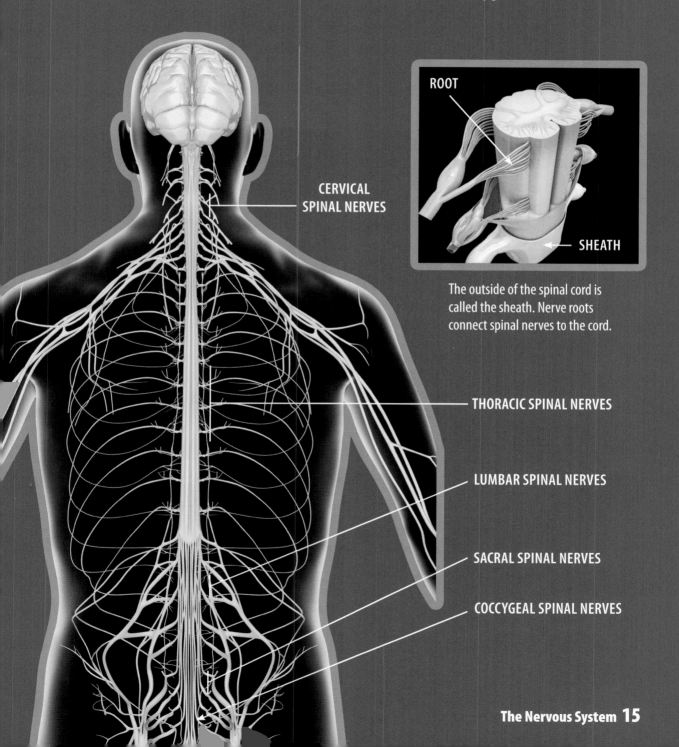

CERVICAL SPINAL NERVES

ROOT

SHEATH

The outside of the spinal cord is called the sheath. Nerve roots connect spinal nerves to the cord.

THORACIC SPINAL NERVES

LUMBAR SPINAL NERVES

SACRAL SPINAL NERVES

COCCYGEAL SPINAL NERVES

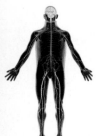

The Torso and Neck

Most of the spinal nerves run through the neck or torso. These spinal nerves branch into many smaller nerves that extend to different areas around the body. Motor nerves carry messages to muscles and glands. Sensory nerves send signals to the central nervous system. Mixed nerves do both jobs.

The Autonomic Nervous System at Work

Nerves of the autonomic nervous system that control many important body functions are located in the torso. These include the nerves regulating movement of the diaphragm and other muscles in the chest that help with breathing. In the **abdomen**, autonomic nerves can detect when the **bladder** is full. Other nerves operate muscles in the large intestine to rid the body of waste.

Nerves in the torso and neck carry a large portion of all the messages that are transmitted between the central and peripheral nervous systems.

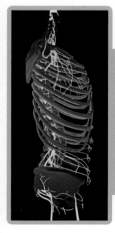

The TORSO AND NECK by the Numbers

1–2 The first two cervical nerves (called C1 and C2) control the head.

8 The eighth cervical nerve (C8) controls the hands.

11 Eleven pairs of thoracic nerves are found between ribs.

Diagram of Torso and Neck Nerves

The different parts of the nervous system work with the body's other systems. The cervical nerves known as C3 and C4 help control the diaphragm, a sheet of muscle between the chest and the abdomen that plays an important role in breathing. When nerves make the diaphragm contract, or tighten up, the size of the chest cavity increases. This helps air flow into the lungs. Signals from nerves then make the diaphragm relax. This reduces the size of the chest cavity, helping to force air out of the lungs.

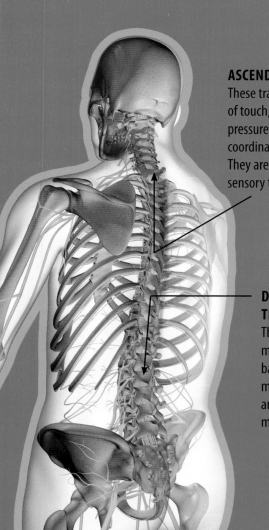

ASCENDING TRACTS
These tracts carry messages of touch, pain, temperature, pressure, body position, and coordination to the brain. They are also known as sensory tracts.

DESCENDING TRACTS
These tracts carry messages about balance and muscle movement. They are also known as motor tracts.

MENINGES

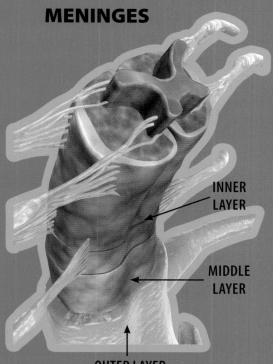

INNER LAYER

MIDDLE LAYER

OUTER LAYER

Ascending and descending tracts run throughout the torso in the spinal cord. The meninges protecting the spinal cord have three layers.

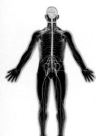

Arms, Hands, Legs, and Feet

The nerves of the arm and hand control their movements. These nerves also receive many messages from sensory neurons. Several nerves branch off from cervical and thoracic spinal nerves to extend into the shoulders and arms.

The radial nerve runs down the back and outside of the upper arm. It works with muscles that straighten the elbow, as well as straighten and lift the fingers, thumb, and wrist. The median nerve extends down the inside of the arm and into the hand. It controls muscles in the hand and forearm. The ulnar nerve is located on the inside of the arm, passing behind the elbow. It connects to muscles that bend the fingers and wrist and also move the fingers from side to side.

The nerves of the leg include the femoral nerve. It transmits messages to muscles in the thigh and lower leg. The longest branch of the femoral nerve is the saphenous nerve, which extends into the foot and small toes. The sciatic nerve runs through the buttock and thigh into the lower leg and foot. The tibial nerve branches from the sciatic nerve.

FUNNY BONE

When bumped at the back of the elbow, people often feel pain shooting down the forearm. This area of the elbow is called the funny bone, because it is near a bone in the upper arm called the humerus. The bone's name sounds like the word *humorous*, which means "funny." When people hit their "funny bone," they are actually hitting the ulnar nerve.

Diagrams of Arms, Hands, Legs, and Feet Nerves

The hands are among the most sensitive areas of the body. They are able to make both delicate and powerful movements. There are about 50 nerves in the hand, branching off the radial, median, and ulnar nerves. There are 200,000 motor neurons controlling hand muscles. Overall, the skin has more than 4 million sensory neurons. Many of those are in the fingertips.

Arm and Hand

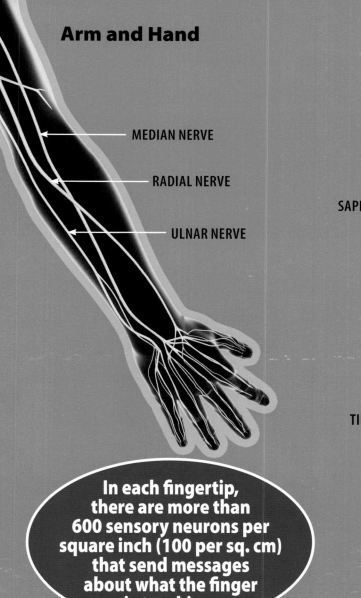

MEDIAN NERVE

RADIAL NERVE

ULNAR NERVE

Leg and Foot

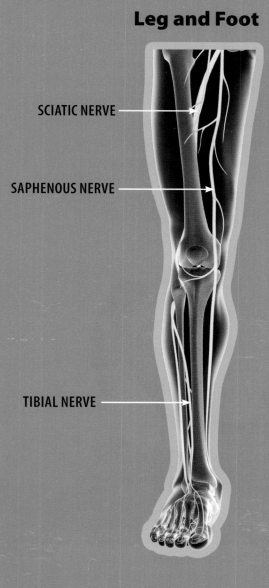

SCIATIC NERVE

SAPHENOUS NERVE

TIBIAL NERVE

In each fingertip, there are more than 600 sensory neurons per square inch (100 per sq. cm) that send messages about what the finger is touching.

Keeping Healthy

The nervous system controls the body's other systems. Therefore, it is important to take care of the nervous system. People can get regular exercise and eat certain foods to help keep their nervous systems working well.

Healthful Foods

Foods rich in vitamins B6, B12, and D are good for the nervous system. Each of these vitamins helps the brain and nerves function properly. Vitamin B6 is found in foods such as chicken, turkey, potatoes, spinach, bananas, and avocados. Foods rich in vitamin B12 include beef, lamb, shrimp, and yogurt. Vitamin D comes from foods such as beef liver, cheese, and egg yolks. It is also added to almost all milk sold in the United States. The body can make vitamin D if a person is outdoors in bright sunlight for at least 15 minutes. Vitamins B6, B12, and D are also found in many fish, such as cod, halibut, salmon, mackerel, and tuna.

Exercise

Regular exercise is good for the nervous system, especially outdoors in fresh air. At least 30 minutes of exercise three times a week is helpful. Ideally, people should exercise for 60 minutes daily.

Exercising outdoors can also give the body a chance to produce vitamin D.

HIGH IN VITAMINS

MILK

SALMON

BANANAS

YOGURT

3 symptoms of meningitis are:
- high fever
- headache
- stiff neck

1 MILLION is the number of Americans who have **Parkinson's disease.**

Nervous System Diseases

Meningitis is an infection usually caused by bacteria or viruses. The meninges covering the brain and spinal cord become inflamed. Permanent injury to the brain may result. Epilepsy is a brain disease that causes people to have seizures. These may include shaking, abnormal behavior, and loss of consciousness.

Multiple sclerosis, or MS, causes messages from the brain to other parts of the body to be blocked. This can lead to vision problems, weakness, and difficulties with walking and balance.

Parkinson's disease is a disorder that causes tremors, or shaking, as well as stiffness and loss of movement. The boxer Muhammad Ali is one of its victims.

Studying the Nervous System

The study of the nervous system is called neurology. Neurologists are doctors who treat diseases and conditions of the nervous system. Doctors and other scientists have been studying the human brain and nervous system since ancient times.

UNDERSTANDING THE BRAIN

About 400 BC The Greek physician Hippocrates writes *On the Sacred Disease*. In this work, he identifies epilepsy, then known as the sacred disease, as a brain disorder.

1600s BC

The brain and nervous system are described in writings from ancient Egypt known as the Edwin Smith Surgical Papyrus.

129 to 216 AD

The Greek physician Galen of Pergamum studies the human body and its systems.

1868

In France, Jean-Martin Charcot is the first doctor to recognize multiple sclerosis as a distinct disease.

1929

Hans Berger develops the electroencephalograph (EEG), a device to record electric currents generated by the brain.

1543

Belgian physician Andreas Vesalius publishes *On the Fabric of the Human Body*, which includes descriptions of the nervous system.

1664

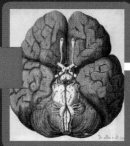

In England, Thomas Willis publishes *Anatomy of the Brain*, followed by *Cerebral Pathology* 12 years later. He studies the brain and describes epilepsy and other disorders.

1817

British scientist James Parkinson writes *An Essay on the Shaking Palsy*, describing the disease that will later bear his name.

1859

Physician John Hughlings Jackson begins working at London Hospital. His studies of nervous-system disorders are among the foundations of modern neurology.

The first images of the brain are made using computed axial tomography (CAT) scanning machines.

The U.S. Food and Drug Administration approves the use of a new medication for a severe form of epilepsy.

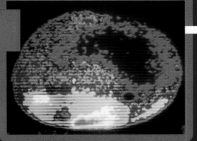

1970s

1970s

2014

Paul Lauterbur develops nuclear magnetic resonance imaging (MRI) technology, now used to detect nervous system diseases.

Working Together

The nervous system plays an important role in the functioning of other body systems. Electrical messages from the brain give instructions to organs and muscles in all parts of the body. Hormones produced in the hypothalamus also keep the body working properly.

The Hypothalamus and the Pituitary Gland

The pituitary **gland**, located at the base of the brain, is part of the endocrine system. Hormones produced in the pituitary gland are important for many body functions. However, the pituitary does not produce these hormones until it receives messages from the hypothalamus to do so. For example, growth hormone from the pituitary gland regulates the growth of muscles and bones. A "releasing" hormone made in the hypothalamus and sent to the pituitary signals the gland that growth hormone is needed.

The entire body is involved when someone shoots a basketball. A part of the brain called the pyramidal tract "tells" the muscles the sequence of movements that are needed.

Controlling the Heart

The accelerans nerves deliver messages from the brain to the heart. When someone is doing strenuous exercise, the accelerans nerve system signals the heart to beat faster. It sends the same signal when a person is anxious or afraid. When physical activity is over or a person no longer feels fear, messages from another set of nerves slow down the heartbeat.

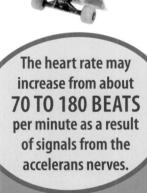

The nervous system makes a skateboarder's heart beat faster to prepare the body's muscles for a jump.

7 HORMONES from the hypothalamus are carried by the blood to the pituitary gland.

The heart rate may increase from about **70 TO 180 BEATS** per minute as a result of signals from the accelerans nerves.

More Than One

The skeletal system and nervous system work closely together. Muscles move bones, but muscles will act only when they receive signals to do so from the brain. Cranial bones of the skeletal system are always protecting the brain from injury. Other bones do the same for the spinal cord.

Careers

Several types of medical professionals study the nervous system or work with patients who have nervous system disorders. When considering careers, it is important to research options and learn about the educational requirements of different professions. It is helpful also to understand what the workday involves in various occupations.

Neurologist

Education
- College degree
- Medical school
- Residency program

Tools

Reflex Hammer

Neurologists diagnose and treat brain diseases or injuries. They also help patients with disorders of the spinal cord or other parts of the nervous system. When neurologists examine patients, they may check muscle strength, movement, balance, **reflexes**, memory, and speech. They also use CAT scans or MRI images to help locate the cause of a problem. Many nervous system disorders have similar symptoms, making it more difficult for doctors to identify the specific cause of each patient's condition.

Education
Neurologists usually study science in college. After graduating, they attend medical school for four years and obtain an MD (doctor of medicine) degree. They then receive specialized training in neurology during a three-year **residency** program.

Physiatrists, also known as rehabilitation physicians, are doctors who work with patients suffering from pain or limited movement as a result of nervous system diseases or injuries. Physiatrists develop a treatment plan for

Physiatrist

Education

- 4 years of college
- 4 years of medical school
- Advanced training

Tools

Weights

each patient that does not involve surgery. The plan, which may include exercises, is intended to help the patient function in his or her daily life.

Education

After obtaining an undergraduate degree, physiatrists study at medical school for four years. They obtain specialized training in a residency program.

Radiologic Technologist

Education

- 2-year college degree
- MRI training
- Continuing education

Tools

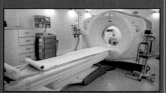

CAT Scan Machine

Radiologic technologists operate equipment that produces images of the body to help doctors diagnose nervous system disorders. This equipment includes X-ray, CAT scan, and MRI machines.

Education

Radiologic technologists usually learn the skills required to operate imaging machinery at two-year colleges. MRI technologists often receive further training. During their careers, technologists must keep their skills up to date as technology changes.

The Nervous System Quiz

Test your knowledge of the nervous system by answering these questions. The answers are provided below for easy reference.

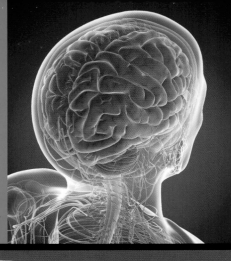

1 What is the weight of an adult's brain?

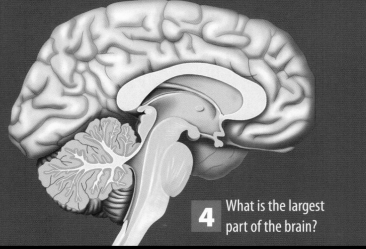

4 What is the largest part of the brain?

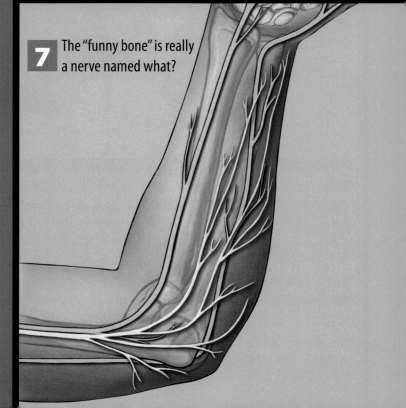

7 The "funny bone" is really a nerve named what?

2 Who was the first doctor to recognize multiple sclerosis as a distinct disease?

3 How many neurons are in the spinal cord?

6 What is another name for efferent neurons?

5 Which vitamin can the body produce from sunlight?

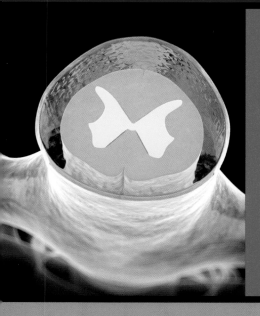

8 What is the name for the clear fluid that surrounds the organs of the central nervous system?

9 Which part of the brain sends signals to the pituitary gland to produce hormones?

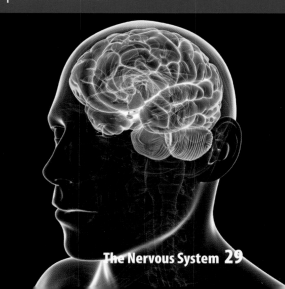

10 How many pairs of spinal nerves does a person have?

Activity

Reflexes protect the body automatically and help people avoid injury. For example, if you place your hand on something very hot, you quickly pull your hand away. Your brain has told your hand to move before you can even think about what is happening.

CHECKING REFLEXES

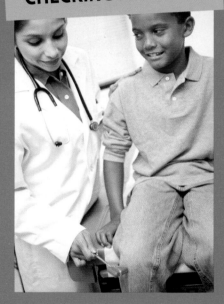

You may have had a test at a doctor's office where the doctor gently hits your knee just below the kneecap. The tap causes your leg to kick out. This is known as the monosynaptic reflex. The doctor is checking how quickly messages travel through your nervous system.

Learn about Reflexes

You can do a simple activity to study how the brain and nervous system affect movement and how reflexes work.

1. Ask your teacher to team up with you for this activity.

2. When the teacher asks you to, stand up at the front of the classroom.

3. Begin talking about the nervous system.

4. Suddenly, slam a book on a table or desk to create a loud noise.

5. The teacher or you should then record the reactions of the other students.

6. Count how many twitched, moved their heads, blinked their eyes, put up their hands, or even screamed.

7. Ask the other students whether they thought about their actions or responded automatically.

Key Words

abdomen: the part of the body between the chest and the pelvis

bladder: an organ of the excretory system that stores urine until it can be eliminated from the body

cells: the smallest structures in the body able to perform the functions necessary for life

connective tissue: body structures that support other body parts

cranium: the part of the skull that encloses the brain

gland: a group of cells or an organ that produces and releases substances for use in the body

hormones: substances in the body that influence the way the body grows and functions

organs: parts of the body that perform special functions

reflexes: body movements and responses that happen without the person thinking about them, such as coughing, blinking, sneezing, or removing a hand from a hot surface

residency: a period, often soon after graduation from medical school, when a doctor receives advanced training by practicing under the supervision of more experienced doctors

sensory organs: the organs of the body related to sight, sound, smell, taste, and touch

tissues: structures in the body made up of the same type of cells

torso: the main part of the body, not including the head, neck, arms, and legs

Index

autonomic nervous system 6, 16
axons 11

brain 4, 6, 7, 8, 9, 10, 11, 12, 13, 14, 17, 21, 22, 23, 24, 25, 26, 28, 29, 30

central nervous system 4, 6, 8, 16, 29
cerebrospinal fluid 8, 12

dendrites 11

epilepsy 21, 22, 23

heart 6, 9, 25
hypothalamus 12, 24, 25

meninges 8, 17, 21
meningitis 21
multiple sclerosis 21, 22, 29

neuroglia 8
neurologist 22, 26
neurons 4, 5, 8, 10, 11, 12, 18, 19, 29

Parkinson's disease 21, 23

peripheral nervous system 4, 6, 8, 11, 16
physiatrist 27

radiologic technologist 27

sensory organs 4, 6, 9, 10
spinal cord 4, 6, 7, 9, 11, 12, 13, 14, 15, 17, 21, 25, 26, 29
synapses 11

vertebrae 9, 14
vitamins 20, 21

The Nervous System **31**

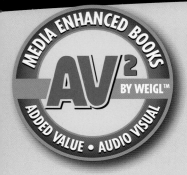

Log on to www.av2books.com

AV² by Weigl brings you media enhanced books that support active learning. Go to www.av2books.com, and enter the special code found on page 2 of this book. You will gain access to enriched and enhanced content that supplements and complements this book. Content includes video, audio, weblinks, quizzes, a slide show, and activities.

AV² Online Navigation

Audio
Listen to sections of the book read aloud.

Book Pages
AV² pages directly correspond to pages in the book.

Video
Watch informative video clips.

Key Words
Study vocabulary, and complete a matching word activity.

Embedded Weblinks
Gain additional information for research.

Quizzes
Test your knowledge.

Slide Show
View images and captions, and prepare a presentation.

Try This!
Complete activities and hands-on experiments.

AV² was built to bridge the gap between print and digital. We encourage you to tell us what you like and what you want to see in the future.

Sign up to be an AV² Ambassador at www.av2books.com/ambassador.